William Sherman

Union General

Colonial Leaders

Lord Baltimore
English Politician and Colonist

Cotton Mather
Author, Clergyman, and Scholar

Miles Standish
Plymouth Colony Leader

Benjamin Banneker
American Mathematician and Astronomer

Increase Mather
Clergyman and Scholar

Peter Stuyvesant
Dutch Military Leader

Sir William Berkeley
Governor of Virginia

James Oglethorpe
Humanitarian and Soldier

George Whitefield
Clergyman and Scholar

William Bradford
Governor of Plymouth Colony

William Penn
Founder of Democracy

Roger Williams
Founder of Rhode Island

Jonathan Edwards
Colonial Religious Leader

Sir Walter Raleigh
English Explorer and Author

John Winthrop
Politician and Statesman

Benjamin Franklin
American Statesman, Scientist, and Writer

Caesar Rodney
American Patriot

John Peter Zenger
Free Press Advocate

Anne Hutchinson
Religious Leader

John Smith
English Explorer and Colonist

Revolutionary War Leaders

John Adams
Second U.S. President

John Hancock
President of the Continental Congress

Francis Marion
The Swamp Fox

Ethan Allen
Revolutionary Hero

Patrick Henry
American Statesman and Speaker

James Monroe
American Statesman

Benedict Arnold
Traitor to the Cause

John Jay
First Chief Justice of the Supreme Court

Thomas Paine
Political Writer

King George III
English Monarch

Thomas Jefferson
Author of the Declaration of Independence

Paul Revere
American Patriot

Nathanael Greene
Military Leader

John Paul Jones
Father of the U.S. Navy

Betsy Ross
American Patriot

Nathan Hale
Revolutionary Hero

Lafayette
French Freedom Fighter

George Washington
First U.S. President

Alexander Hamilton
First U.S. Secretary of the Treasury

James Madison
Father of the Constitution

Famous Figures of the Civil War Era

Jefferson Davis
Confederate President

Robert E. Lee
Confederate General

Sojourner Truth
Abolitionist, Suffragist, and Preacher

Frederick Douglass
Abolitionist and Author

Abraham Lincoln
Civil War President

Harriet Tubman
Leader of the Underground Railroad

Ulysses S. Grant
Military Leader and President

William Sherman
Union General

Stonewall Jackson
Confederate General

Harriet Beecher Stowe
Author of Uncle Tom's Cabin

William Sherman

Union General

Henna Remstein

Arthur M. Schlesinger, jr.
Senior Consulting Editor

Chelsea House Publishers

Philadelphia

Produced by 21st Century Publishing and Communications, Inc.
New York, NY. http://www.21cpc.com

CHELSEA HOUSE PUBLISHERS
Production Manager Pamela Loos
Art Director Sara Davis
Director of Photography Judy L. Hasday
Managing Editor James D. Gallagher
Senior Production Editor J. Christopher Higgins

Staff for *WILLIAM SHERMAN*
Project Editor Anne Hill
Associate Art Director Takeshi Takahashi
Series Design Keith Trego

The Chelsea House World Wide Web address is
http://www.chelseahouse.com

First Printing
1 3 5 7 9 8 6 4 2

Library of Congress Cataloging-in-Publication Data

Remstein, Henna, 1968–
    William Sherman / Henna R. Remstein.
        p.   cm. — (Famous figures of the Civil War era)
    Includes bibliographical references and index.
    ISBN 0-7910-6005-5 (HC) — ISBN 0-7910-6143-4 (PB)
        1. Sherman, William T. (William Tecumseh), 1820–1891—Juvenile
literature. 2. Generals—United States—Biography—Juvenile literature.
3. United States. Army—Biography—Juvenile literature. 4. United States—
History—Civil War, 1861–1865—Campaigns—Juvenile literature.
[1. Sherman, William T. (William Tecumseh), 1820–1891. 2. Generals.
3. United States—History—Civil War, 1861–1865.] I. Title. II. Series.

E467.1.S55 R46 2000
355'.0092—dc21
[B]   00-038378
                                                            CIP

Publisher's Note: In Colonial, Revolutionary War, and Civil War Era
America, there were no standard rules for spelling, punctuation,
capitalization, or grammar. Some of the quotations that appear in
the Colonial Leaders, Revolutionary War Leaders, and Famous
Figures of the Civil War Era series come from original documents
and letters written during this time in history. Original quotations
reflect writing inconsistencies of the period.

Contents

Small towns and villages like this one were scattered along the Ohio frontier where William T. Sherman was born. When tragedy struck with the death of his father, the boy's life changed, setting him on the path his future life would take.

Childhood Tragedy

Charles and Mary Sherman of Lancaster, Ohio, chose an unusual name for their sixth child. When their little son was born on February 8, 1820, his parents named him Tecumseh. Settlers in Ohio knew the name very well. Tecumseh was a famous Native American warrior and leader of the Shawnee tribe. Many people, including the little boy's father, admired Tecumseh, who was known as a peacemaker and for his battle skills.

Tecumseh Sherman lived in a two-story house with a large, loving family that included 10 brothers and sisters. All 10 called the middle boy "Cump," a

The man for whom Tecumseh Sherman was named was a great Indian warrior. A chief of the Shawnee tribe, his followers also called him Shooting Star. Tall, handsome, and wise, Tecumseh wanted peace with white settlers. But when peace was not possible, he gathered many tribes and fought the settlers along the frontier. But Tecumseh could not win. At a battle with an American army in 1813, he was shot and killed. His body was never found.

nickname that stayed with him the rest of his life.

Lancaster was on the Ohio **frontier,** which was mostly wilderness. Even though the town was small, it was big enough to have a schoolhouse, a jail, and a courthouse. Charles Sherman was a lawyer who served as a judge on the Ohio Supreme Court, the highest court in the state.

When Cump was nine years old, tragedy struck the family. His father became seriously ill while working far from home at a court in Ohio. After suffering with a fever for several days, he died on June 24, 1829. Life for Cump and the other Sherman children would change forever.

Tecumseh's mother could not support the family on her own, and she was forced to turn

William hunted and fished in the hills around Lancaster. He also enjoyed games with his friends. Being athletic, he most likely played the rough and tumble game of "snap the whip."

over the care of her children to friends and relatives. Some were as far away as the city of Cincinnati, Ohio. But Cump, who was easily spotted around town with his bright red hair, stayed close to home and familiar surroundings. He moved one block up the street to live with Thomas Ewing, a lawyer, his wife Maria, and their six children.

Young William got his early education in a frontier schoolroom much like this one. Reading, writing, and arithmetic were basic subjects, and William was said to excel in math and languages.

The Ewings treated Cump as one of their own, and he soon became best friends with the oldest Ewing son, Philemon. The two boys, only eight months apart in age, roamed the nearby hills, swam and fished in the Hocking River, and enjoyed sledding and snowball fights in the winter. Cump went to school with Phil and the other Ewing children, John and Ellen. Thomas Ewing later wrote that Cump was athletic and a good scholar, particularly in math and languages.

Cump's new foster mother, Maria, was a devout Roman Catholic, and she wanted the boy to be baptized in the Catholic Church. At the baptism, the priest gave Cump a religious name– William, in honor of Saint William. From then on, the teenager signed his name W. T. or William T. Sherman, but his friends still called him Cump.

When William was 16, his life changed in a way that would put him on the path to a lifetime of military service. When his foster father, Thomas Ewing, was elected to the United States Senate, he was able to get William an appointment to the U.S. Military Academy at West Point.

A t the age of six, Cump earned his first "battle" scar. Each night, when Charles Sherman rode home from work on horseback, the Sherman children raced to reach their father's horse. The winner rode the horse to the barn. Usually, one of the older children earned this honor. The night young Cump beat out his brothers and sisters, the horse threw him to the ground. He recovered from his injuries, but a scar on his face could be seen for the rest of his life.

Officers review an artillery unit of the U.S. army, which was the branch assigned to William when he graduated from West Point. He had wanted to be in the Army Corps of Engineers, but he made the best of his early disappointment and held several posts in the South.

Early Disappointment

The United States Military Academy, known as West Point, is located along the Hudson River in New York State. The academy was founded in 1802 to give young men an education and train them to be officers in the U.S. army. William entered as a **cadet**, and when he graduated after four years of study, he would be a second lieutenant in the army.

Although William excelled in his studies at West Point, he often broke the strict rules of the academy. Sometimes the teenager missed roll call when attendance was taken. Other times, he turned up wearing dirty clothes. Young men training for the army were expected to obey orders, one of which was to be spotlessly clean at all times.

William had many friends among his classmates, some of whom would later serve under his command in the army. He enjoyed entertaining his friends at late night feasts, which he organized himself. William sometimes served meals of oysters, potatoes, and butter and bread that he had obtained without permission. Because of his sometimes undisciplined behavior and mischievous antics, William accumulated numerous **demerits** during his four years at West Point.

In 1840, after doing very well on his final exams, William graduated sixth in his class. Still, because of his demerits, he was not offered a post with the Army Corps of Engineers, which was considered one of the best army groups. Instead the army offered William a choice. He could join the artillery branch, which managed guns and cannons. Or he could be an officer in the infantry, the branch that trains and organizes soldiers to fight on foot. Second Lieutenant William Sherman chose artillery and joined the Third Artillery Regiment in Fort Pierce, Florida.

He arrived there at the end of the Second Seminole War, a series of conflicts from 1835 to 1842 between army forces and the Florida Seminole Indians. The U.S. government wanted to remove the Seminoles from their lands in Florida, and the Indians fought back. Many did surrender and moved west into Indian Territory. Others refused to give up and retreated deep into the Florida Everglades. The Second Seminole War was an attempt by the army to finally remove the Indians from Florida.

Because the conflict was coming to an end when William arrived, the battles were minor and few, and he did not see much action. For a young, eager army officer, the lack of fighting was boring. Living conditions were also poor, with officers staying in primitive cabins at the fort. Since William's daily duties were simple, he spent much of his time with other officers catching turtles and fishing.

In 1841, William was promoted to the higher rank of first lieutenant and was assigned to a series of army posts. He served in St. Augustine, Florida, and then went to Fort Morgan, Alabama. Finally, he was assigned to Fort Moultrie, near Charleston, South Carolina.

During the time William spent in the South, he gained insight into the **culture** and traditions of the region. He became very fond of the relaxed and polite society of the city of Charleston. He also saw, probably for the first time, how the practice of **slavery** worked in the states of the South.

Although the South had a few large cities like Charleston, it was mainly a region of farms and large **plantations**. To work the thousands of acres of fields, Southerners used African people and made them slaves. Decades before, farmers had bought Africans who had been captured in

Serving in the South, William saw firsthand scenes of slaves picking cotton in the fields of large plantations. William sympathized with the needs of Southern farmers for workers, and he did not speak out against slavery.

their native country and carried across the ocean on ships by slave traders. The Africans and their children became slaves and were forced to work for their owners.

While difficult to imagine, slavery was an accepted form of labor in the southern United States. Slave owners defended slavery, declaring it was necessary because their way of life depended on farming. The major crop in the South was cotton, and it had to be planted, picked, and processed. This was the work of the majority of slaves. William believed Southern farmers needed slaves to work in their fields, and he did not question whether it was right or wrong.

But in the North, many did question slavery. Known as **abolitionists**, these Northerners believed slavery was wrong and had no place in the United States. Their opposition to slavery angered Southerners, who were determined to keep their slaves.

Another intense debate of the time centered around the rights of individual states in the United States. Many Southerners believed that the rights of states were above the laws and rules set down in the U.S. Constitution. They felt that the government in Washington, D.C., was too powerful. Although William did not openly oppose slavery, he often discussed the issue of states' rights. He did not agree that the rights of states were above the Constitution.

During his time at Fort Moultrie, William became engaged to 19-year-old Ellen Boyle Ewing, the eldest daughter of his foster parents. But they would not be married for several years. In 1845, the United States went to war with Mexico over the boundary line between the two nations. As an army officer, William was called to duty.

Most of the fighting of the Mexican War took place in Mexico, where the U.S. army won several battles. But there was some fighting in California, which was then owned by Mexico. American settlers in California rose up against the Mexican government and declared themselves independent.

To help the settlers in California, a U.S. army unit marched into California, and William was among its officers. Most of the fighting was over by the time William arrived, and again he saw little action. Much of his job consisted of paperwork and managing supplies. Since he had plenty of leisure time, he hunted, took a drawing class, and taught himself to paint. Still, he was disappointed not to be in action. He found his life there lonely, and he missed Ellen.

By 1848, the Mexican War was over, and William spent the next two years in the cities of San Francisco and Sacramento, California. Finally, after a seven-year engagement, 30-year-old William returned to marry Ellen at the Ewing house in Washington, D.C., on May 1, 1850. The tall, slim bridegroom was dashing in a fresh new uniform with his sword at his side and spurs on his boots. An honored guest at the wedding was President Zachary Taylor, who was accompanied by numerous U.S. senators.

That fall, William was promoted to captain. A few months later, on January 18, 1851, Ellen gave birth to their first child, daughter Maria Ewing. The couple eventually had eight children, three more girls and four boys.

William moved his wife and new baby to

Saying good-bye to loved ones was hard for army officers. William did not want to leave his family behind. Instead, he resigned from the army, working at several different jobs around the country.

St. Louis, Missouri, where he served with the army's Third Artillery unit at Jefferson Barracks. He also managed his father-in-law's properties to earn extra money. After a year and a half in St. Louis, William resigned from the army. With a second baby on the way, he realized he could not support his growing family on a captain's salary.

Throughout the 1850s, William jumped from job to job and state to state. In San Francisco, he began working in a bank, and as he was promoted to a better job, he and Ellen lived a comfortable and elegant life. In 1855, he was nominated for city treasurer but decided not to run for the position. Then, misfortune struck when California's economy collapsed and the bank closed. William was jobless.

For a year and a half afterward, William and Ellen lived in Leavenworth, Kansas. William managed Ewing family property, set up a farm, and sold insurance. The highlight of his experience in Kansas was being admitted to the practice of law by the Kansas Bar Association. After practicing law for a time in Kansas, William and Ellen lived briefly in New York

City. Finally he and his growing family settled in Louisiana, where William became the head of the Louisiana State Seminary of Learning and Military Academy, a new school for boys that opened on January 2, 1860.

Around the same time, William began to worry about the growing tensions between the North and the South over the issues of slavery and states' rights. The majority of people in the North opposed slavery. Northerners, especially the abolitionists, wrote and spoke out strongly against it. Most Southerners supported slavery, seeing it as a necessity to maintain their farms and plantations.

In 1860, the North and the South began to split apart. Abraham Lincoln, who opposed slavery, was elected president. Southerners feared that Lincoln would act to end slavery, and many began to argue that they should **secede** from the United States and form an independent nation.

By 1861, the North and the South were so

When William knew war was coming, he was convinced that it would be long and bloody. He was very concerned that the North was not properly prepared. In a meeting with President Lincoln shortly before the war began, he stated his strong concerns. To William, Lincoln seemed weak when he replied, "Oh well! I guess we'll manage to keep house." Highly disappointed, William left the White House angry with all politicians. Later, William came to admire Lincoln, feeling the president was as much a soldier as he was a political leader.

deeply divided that no **compromise** seemed possible. South Carolina had already seceded, and Mississippi, Florida, Alabama, Georgia, Louisiana, and Texas followed. Within weeks, Virginia, Arkansas, North Carolina, and Tennessee also left the United States. President Lincoln refused to recognize these **Confederate States of America** as an independent nation, and the terrible **Civil War** between the North and South began.

Although William did believe that Southerners had a right to own slaves, he also believed the South was wrong to oppose the laws of the U.S. Constitution. He knew his duty was to the

Union, and now it was time to go home to Lancaster, Ohio. William was sad that he had to leave his friends in Louisiana. Before he left, he spoke with them, saying: "You're driving me and hundreds of others out of the South who've cast our fortunes here and love your people and want to stay. Yet I must give it all up . . . and once war comes, as it surely will, I must fight you."

When he arrived in Lancaster, he found a letter from the War Department in Washington, D.C., asking him to rejoin the army. He would have the rank of colonel in command of his own regiment. William Tecumseh Sherman was going to lead Northern soldiers against the South.

Called back into action when the Civil War broke out, William (front row, second from left) at last was going into battle. Here, with other Northern generals, he rides at the right of a hatless General Ulysses S. Grant, future commander of the U.S. army.

Into Battle
and Beyond

Each side in the Civil War had a **strategy** which it hoped would end the war quickly. Northern forces would invade the South and try to capture its cities, especially the Confederate capital of Richmond, Virginia. The South would defend its territory and drive Northern armies back. The first battle using this strategy took place on July 21, 1861, when Union troops marched into Virginia. They formed their lines along a creek called Bull Run and waited for Southern forces to fight.

As a colonel of the Union's 13th Regular Infantry, William finally got his chance to fight at Bull Run.

Marching with his unit from Washington, D.C., William confronted the Confederates. Like many other Union officers, William was not yet an experienced military leader. Also, Union soldiers had not yet had very much training. Mostly all volunteers, they did not know how to fight very well and would not hold their ground, William reported later.

Still, William led his men bravely and fought fiercely. Bullets flew all around him, and his horse was shot out from under him. William tried to rally his men, but there was too much confusion. Many soldiers began fleeing from the battlefield. Bull Run was a great disaster for the Union forces, who finally had no choice but to retreat to Washington in terrible defeat.

The lost battle made a deep and lasting impression on William. For the first time, he saw the tremendous ugliness of war. He later described his feelings at seeing the dead, dismembered, and wounded men and horses, scattered all over the battlefield. He wrote:

"At one point I could see the entire [destruction] of battle, men lying in every [sort of] shape and mangled in horrible ways. . . ."

But the Union army was not ready to give up just yet. Northern forces continued to push into Virginia, winning some important battles and losing others. At the same time, Union forces began invading the western states of Tennessee and Mississippi. The North's plan was to gain control of the Mississippi River and cut off Texas, Arkansas, and Louisiana from the rest of the Confederacy.

In January 1862, President Lincoln approved William's promotion to brigadier general. William left the war in the East and headed west, where he was assigned to support the forces of Brigadier General Ulysses S. Grant, who was attacking Confederate forces in Tennessee. By March, William was put in charge of his own division in the Union forces in Tennessee as Grant prepared for a major battle.

The great battle came in April at a place

called Shiloh in southwestern Tennessee. A large force of Confederate soldiers surprised Grant and William and nearly defeated them. At the first sign that Confederate troops were approaching, William did nothing. He did not believe there would be a general attack on his position. Later, newspapers criticized William for not moving quickly and for ignoring standard military procedures, such as digging trenches along the front lines.

Despite hesitating at first, William triumphed when the battle finally came. During the first day, both sides attacked and retreated, with neither gaining very much ground. The morning of the second day, General Grant ordered William to take the offensive–to attack the other side first instead of sitting and waiting to defend against an enemy attack.

William obeyed, and though wounded twice, he showed great skill and leadership. He gained the trust and respect of his soldiers as well as praise from General Grant. In his written report,

Grant praised the judgment and bravery William showed on the battlefield at Shiloh. Grant also wrote to his wife that "In General Sherman, the country has an able and [brave] defender. . . ." From that point on General Grant considered the 41-year-old William to be his right-hand man.

Reports of the battle swept through the divided nation, and both generals were hailed as heroes in the North. But many newspaper reporters also wrote articles blaming Grant and Sherman for the terrible Union losses at Shiloh. The papers said that Grant and Sherman were not prepared and that the generals were completely surprised by the attack. William was furious. He wrote an angry letter to his brother John, who was a U.S. Senator, claiming the reports were false. From that time on, William hated newspaper reporters.

Soon after the battle at Shiloh, Union General Henry W. Halleck arrived and took away General Grant's active command. Halleck and

Like most other Civil War generals, William did not like newspaper reporters, believing that most were liars. Not only did they criticize his ability and character, their reports of battle plans some-times fell into enemy hands. When Confederates got some maps sent by one young reporter, William exploded. Accusing the reporter of spying, he had him arrested and held for a military trial. The young man was found not guilty, but he was forbidden to ever come to a battlefield again.

Grant did not get along, and Halleck seemed to believe the newspaper stories. Terribly upset and thinking he would never get command of another division, Grant almost left the army. William may have helped Grant through this difficult time by making him promise not to leave or by tearing up his letter of resignation.

Grant recovered how-ever, and by the summer of 1862 had again been placed in command of an army, this time in the West. He was making plans to finally defeat Confederate forces and take control of the Mississippi River. Relying on William, Grant sent him to set up a Union base in Memphis, Tennessee. The Confederate city had

Many newspaper reporters camped with the armies and reported on the battles, and often the failures, of officers. Like William, many generals thought the reporters did not treat them fairly, writing only about their mistakes and not their successes.

been captured earlier by Union naval forces.

William found Memphis too quiet. The stores, city offices, schools, and churches were closed. He restored the mayor's office and ordered everything to open. But many residents had abandoned their homes, and others were suffering from the lack of food and other supplies. With occupation by the North, supplies that had been scarce began to flow into the region.

However, William realized that certain supplies—such as guns—could end up in the hands of the Confederate army. To protect the strength of the Union's position, he banned shipping and restricted travel by **civilians**.

In Memphis, William began to think about slavery again. His family and friends in the North felt the general should take a strong stand against slavery. But William was not an abolitionist. He still questioned whether it was right to take slaves from masters who had paid money for them. He also strongly believed that if slaves were freed, they would not be able to feed, clothe, and house themselves.

Still, while in Memphis, William and his officers gave jobs to former slaves, many of whom had run away from their owners. For $10 a month and food, some blacks worked as cooks, while others served as construction workers.

But William was not through with fighting. Part of Grant's plan was to capture the important Confederate stronghold of Vicksburg, Mississippi. He ordered William to leave Memphis and march south toward Vicksburg. At the end of December 1862, William met Confederate forces at Chickasaw Bluffs, north of Vicksburg. William's troops fought under heavy gunfire and in a thick fog. But they could not take the Confederate position high on the bluffs along the river. William retreated.

William's loss was embarrassing, and again newspapers wrote that he lacked ability. But William did capture a Confederate fort at a place called Arkansas Post. There, he was helped by gunboats that floated up the Mississippi River and attacked the fort. William took Arkansas Post within a few hours.

At the end of 1862, William was playing an

When the Union army recruited free African Americans, nearly 200,000 signed up. Many people thought they would not be good soldiers, but blacks fought with great courage in many battles of the Civil War.

important part in General Grant's campaign to capture Vicksburg. The well-protected city sat at a critical bend in the Mississippi River. To defeat

Confederate forces in the West, the Union had to take the city.

For several months in the spring of 1863, General Grant fought back and forth with Confederate troops around Vicksburg. He was trying to wear them down. Finally, in May 1863, Grant laid **siege** to the city.

William watches as his soldiers march off to meet with
Confederate forces. Now a general who had proved his
value to the Union, William was ready to show that he
could lead his men to fight and win battles.

Marching, Fighting, and Winning

eading 33,000 troops, William took part in the battles around Vicksburg and in the siege of the city. Grant tried many approaches to winning the city. William did not always agree with Grant's strategies. He thought that trying to attack Vicksburg directly would not work. Although William argued with his good friend, he followed Grant's orders. One of his most important missions was to attack and scatter Confederate general John Pemberton's forces around Vicksburg. But Confederate forces fought fiercely, and William could not overcome them.

At the same time, the people of Vicksburg were

suffering from the siege. The city was constantly shelled by gunboats in the river. Food and weapons were low. Some fled and lived in caves along the river bank.

Because General Grant's supply base was far away in Memphis, soldiers generally had to feed themselves. They took all the food they could find. This made it even harder for the Southerners to survive.

During the campaign, Union armies destroyed tremendous amounts of property along the Mississippi River. Burning homes, railroads, farms, and warehouses helped break the spirit of the people. The destruction weakened the Confederates and helped contribute to the Union victory in the West.

Finally, on July 4, 1863, Vicksburg surrendered. Newspapers began praising William as an able leader. Though William wanted to be part of the victory celebration, Grant ordered him to Jackson, Mississippi. Late summer heat slowed down William's troops, and he set up camp in August along the banks of the Big Black River.

During a six-week rest, his wife Ellen and four of their children visited him. When Grant ordered William to move again, this time to Chattanooga, Tennessee, he joined his family on first leg of their journey home. They sailed upriver to Memphis, and from there, Ellen and the children would travel back to Lancaster, Ohio.

On board the ship, tragedy struck. William's son Willy became very sick with a fever. When the ship docked, William rushed the boy to a doctor. But it was too late, and little Willy died. William was devastated. He later wrote how Willy's death affected him. "[A]sleep or awake, I saw little Willy as plain as life. I could see him stumbling over the sand hills on Harrison Street in San Francisco. . . . could see him running to meet me with open arms at Big Black River. And last, I could see him moaning as he died."

William was glad when Grant ordered him, along with four army divisions, to Chattanooga, located in eastern Tennessee. Confederate armies still roamed Tennessee. In quick raids, they destroyed towns and railroads and captured many Union soldiers. A large Confederate army was holding Chattanooga, which was an important railroad center. If Union forces could take the city, the road would be open into Georgia.

Conditions on the march were very difficult for William's soldiers. They never had enough food, and they marched in rain and through mud, some times with no shoes. There was not enough clean water because Confederates had polluted the streams and wells. Yet they continued to march.

In the East, other battles raged, including the battle at Gettysburg, Pennsylvania. Gettysburg was considered one of the main turning points of the Civil War. Fought for three days in July 1863, Union troops finally defeated the Army of Virginia. On November 19, 1863, President Abraham Lincoln dedicated the battlefield as a national cemetery. President Lincoln delivered a short but powerful two-minute speech known as the Gettysburg Address. It has become one of the most famous speeches in U.S. history.

This illustration is of the Battle of Gettysburg, the last battle fought on Northern soil. The Confederate defeat here was the turning point in the war.

In the meantime, in Tennessee, Union forces had fought their way into Chattanooga. But Confederate armies surrounded the city, trapping

Union forces inside. In November 1863, other Union armies from the East joined William's divisions around Chattanooga. Grant ordered William to attack a place called Tunnel Hill. It was an important location because a railroad, which could bring supplies to the Confederates, passed through the tunnel.

William was supposed to lead a head-on attack, but he did not. He was skilled at hitting the enemy's flanks, or sides, but not at direct attacks on the front. William fought all day long, but he did not seize Tunnel Hill, even though his troops outnumbered the Confederates. Despite William's failure, Grant still supported him. He praised William for engaging the Confederates so that Union general George Henry Thomas could break through Confederate lines.

Chattanooga was finally taken in November, and the way was open for Union forces to march into Georgia. General Grant gave William the command of three armies in the West. His future mission was to defeat the large army of

Confederate general Joseph Johnston and take the city of Atlanta.

But first, William went home on a visit. He spent the Christmas of 1863 with Ellen and their children. The town's citizens treated him like a famous hero. People came to visit and crowded around him. On New Year's Day 1864, William took his daughter Minnie by train to a boarding school in Cincinnati. He found leaving his family sad but continued on to Memphis. There, he prepared for an expedition into Mississippi.

Although the Union controlled the Mississippi River, some Confederate forces remained in the state. General Grant gave William permission to march 20,000 soldiers through eastern Mississippi and destroy whatever was in his path. William's troops tore up miles of railroads and burned hospitals, offices, warehouses, and homes. They took horses, cattle, and food. On the return march, 6,000 **refugees** followed his troops. Most were former slaves.

Many thought William's way of waging war on civilians was too harsh. Southerners came to

William's soldiers ripped up railroads and burned buildings as they marched through Confederate territory. William firmly believed that such destruction would break the morale of Southerners and force them to surrender.

hate him. But William believed that this was the way to defeat the Confederates and teach them a lesson. He said: "We would make them so sick of war that generations would pass away before they would again appeal to it."

By now, the North had twice as many soldiers and supplies as the South. With most Southern railroads in ruins, the Confederates could not transport food and supplies to soldiers and civilians. At the same time, a Union **blockade** of Southern port cities kept supplies from entering the cities. The Union naval ships were blocking most of the Southern seaports. The South was starving, and its people were losing hope.

Although William commanded Union armies in the West, he had not yet had a major victory. At a meeting with General Grant in Cincinnati, Ohio, William received the orders that would make him famous. He was to march to Atlanta, the South's most important railroad center, and take the city.

O n his march through Georgia, one of William's methods of ruining railroads was making "Sherman's neckties." William ordered his soldiers to dig up the metal rails and soften them up over fires. The soldiers then twisted them around trees. Confederates could not pry them loose, and the Georgia countryside was littered with rails twisted around trees.

Southerners came to regard William, here in a formal portrait, as a "devil" for the destruction he caused in taking Atlanta and because of his famous "March to the Sea" through Georgia.

Taking Atlanta

In the spring of 1864, William set out from his base in Chattanooga. He commanded three armies of around 100,000 soldiers. His army and the other two advanced across Georgia, fighting **skirmishes** along the way and pushing Confederate forces toward Atlanta. William's strategy was to get between the army of Confederate general Joseph Johnston and Atlanta.

Marching across Georgia, William's men cut a path of destruction. Soldiers and homeless followers trampled crops and took food and supplies from the people. But the Union troops were also becoming weakened by the marching and fighting.

At the end of May, William let his soldiers rest, but not for long. By June, his forces had advanced 100 miles toward Atlanta and pushed back the Confederate forces led by General Johnston. When William received **reinforcements**, he began to follow the railroad line between the towns of Acworth and Marietta, Georgia. Reaching Pine Mountain, William did not think Confederate troops were camped out, so he ordered his soldiers to advance.

William was wrong. The Confederates resisted, and William made little progress. In a letter to General Grant, William blamed some of the officers under his command. He complained that they were not aggressive and were too slow.

Then in mid-June, William ordered General Joseph Hooker's troops to seize the town of Marietta. Hooker's forces took the town with very few losses of men. In spite of the win, William could not advance farther for several days. General Johnston's entire Southern army held back the front line of Union troops that stretched 10 miles long.

General Johnston was called "Retreating Joe" because he did not want to face William in a direct battle. Johnston was an excellent general, but he was outnumbered by Union forces and did not have enough guns or cannons. He believed it was best to keep moving toward Atlanta and save his army.

When Johnston did fight, he chose to stand where he thought he could win. William was impatient to take Atlanta, and he made a mistake at a place called Kennesaw Mountain. Confederate troops were dug in behind **entrenchments** on the slope of a hill. William ordered a direct attack with the full force of his army.

The attack made little headway. The day was terribly hot, and hundreds of Union soldiers fell from the heat. From the gunfire, the woods caught fire, and many more men were burned. William lost some 2,000 men while Johnston's

At the Battle of Kennesaw Mountain, William's troops march directly toward entrenched Confederate forces. A direct attack was a mistake, and Union casualties were high.

losses were around 500.

Another attempt to drive Confederate forces toward the Chattahoochee River was also unsuccessful. At this point, both Northern and Southern troops were camped along the banks of the Chattahoochee. The soldiers called a **truce** and began mingling. They shared coffee, tobacco, and bathed side-by-side in the river. Such truces sometimes happened during the Civil War. Soldiers could stop fighting one another for a time and behave as men rather than as enemies.

By July 17, William was within 12 miles of Atlanta. He then learned that Johnston had been replaced by General John Hood. The Confederate government was unhappy with Johnston's constant retreating. During the end of July and through August, William's troops battled with Hood's forces outside Atlanta, often in brutal hand-to-hand combat.

Both sides suffered from the heat and bad food. Ordinary soldiers' food during the Civil War was mainly bread, bacon, and coffee. Without fresh vegetables and fruit, many got sick from the lack of vitamin C, becoming weak and unable to fight well.

William also suffered personally outside Atlanta. One of his generals, his good friend James McPherson, was killed in a fight. William wept when he saw the body of his friend. He wrote to the government of McPherson's death: "History tells us of but few who so blended the grace and gentleness of the friend and the dignity, courage, faith and manliness of the soldier."

Returning to the fighting, William won a victory at a place called Ezra Church. General Hood lost some 5,000 soldiers. Now William realized that victory was near. He sent forces southwest around Atlanta to destroy the railroads around the city. His armies tore up the railroad tracks, cutting off Hood's lines of communication and transportation.

General Hood, whose troops had been protecting Atlanta, thought William had retreated. When he realized Union troops were approaching the city, he ordered an attack, which failed. Hood could not hold out any longer.

On September 1, 1864, Hood began moving his remaining troops out of Atlanta, leaving the city unprotected. As his final act, he ordered Atlanta's stockpile of weapons to be blown up.

William leans on a cannon at the siege line outside Atlanta. The artillery fire directed at the city destroyed much of Atlanta and caused terrified residents to flee from their homes.

He wanted to make sure that William would not benefit from finding a surplus of guns and ammunition.

On September 2, William sent a message to President Lincoln saying that Atlanta was "fairly won." As William and his soldiers marched through the empty streets, the army band played patriotic songs. But most Atlanta residents did not hear the music. Hundreds had fled, and others hid in their homes.

William soon set up strict rules. All remaining residents were ordered to leave unless they pledged their loyalty to the North. He did not want his army slowed down by feeding and caring for civilians. The newspapers judged him as cruel for forcing 446 families to leave.

William had captured Atlanta, but the Civil War raged on. The North needed a new plan to end the war for good—and William believed he had just the idea to do it. He called it a "March to the Sea." Union troops would surge across Georgia, not stopping until they reached the seaport at Savannah. As he had done in Mississippi, William was determined to break down civilians' **morale.** Marching through Georgia would show the Union army's strength and destroy what little remained of Confederate soldiers and supplies.

For William, winning was everything. When he received permission for his March to the Sea,

Union troops enter the empty streets of a Southern town. William and his soldiers were also greeted by mostly empty streets when they marched into towns on their way to coastal Savannah.

he is said to have exclaimed, "I can make Georgia howl." As William left Atlanta, he ordered his troops to bomb homes and buildings. The fires spread quickly, destroying much of the city.

Each day along the march, numerous soldiers were assigned to **forage** for food. They became known as "bummers." William's soldiers also stole food, cattle, clothes, household goods, and jewelry. William did not approve of stealing, but he did not stop it. He knew it would terrify people and that their fear would break their spirits.

Marching 10 to 15 miles a day for 33 days, William and his thousands of troops could be tracked by the stories of destruction. Even President Lincoln did not know from day to day where the troops were headed. When William reached the outskirts of Savannah in December, he found a main bridge had been burned by Confederates. He needed that bridge to get his men across the Ogeechee River.

To rebuild the bridge, William's engineers tore down trees and houses. On December 13, Union soldiers crossed the bridge and captured Fort McAllister, 15 miles outside Savannah. This opened a path for William to move into the city.

When William finally marched into Savannah, the people did not resist. Confederate general William Hardee had fled the city, leaving it to

William. On December 22, 1864, William sent a message to President Lincoln. It said, "I beg to present you, as a Christmas gift, the city of Savannah."

Although William had won Georgia for the Union, his victory was darkened by yet another family tragedy. During the Atlanta campaign, another little son was born to him and his wife. William knew the newborn baby was sick, but he had received no letters or news from home. He had to learn the sad news from a newspaper article that little Charles, the son he never met, had died.

Overcoming his sadness, William began to repair Savannah. He organized a police force and opened schools and stores. For a month, William caught up on his rest and answered his many letters. He also began thinking about the end of the war.

The war was coming to an end when William (left) met with General Grant (center) and President Lincoln. On board the steamer *River Queen*, the three leaders discussed the upcoming peace terms for the South.

An End to
the War

Although the South seemed totally defeated, the war was not yet over. In January 1865, William left Savannah and began his march to Columbia, South Carolina, the state capital. His strategy was to confuse the remaining Confederate forces by splitting up his troops. He sent some to the city of Charleston and some back to Atlanta.

For much of the 45-day march to Columbia, William's troops trudged through rain. They slept in trees rather than on wet ground. After the war, soldiers on this mission called it the "Smokey March." Because they were still under orders to destroy the countryside, Union soldiers burned small towns, farmhouses, stores of cotton, and railroads. Thick smoke filled the sky for miles, sometimes making it difficult for the troops to see and breathe.

Finally arriving outside Columbia, William ordered the city to be bombed by artillery fire. When the mayor surrendered on February 17, the city was burning out of control. Wind and dry conditions fed the flames that raged until 4 A.M. At sunrise, nearly two-thirds of Columbia had burned, and thousands of people were left homeless.

Southerners blamed William for burning Columbia. William insisted that Confederate forces had burned the city as they fled. At one point, a group of angry women met with William at his headquarters, asking why he had set Columbia on fire. William responded by telling them that when Southerners started the war, they were responsible for all the burning and destruction in the South. "The fire they kindled has been burning ever since," he said, "and it reached your houses last night."

After Columbia, William met with President Lincoln and General Grant and received orders for his next mission. Grant was to fight General Robert E. Lee in Virginia. William was to battle once more with General Joseph Johnston who had moved his forces to North Carolina. Because North Carolina was one of the last states to secede from the Union, William felt more sympathy for its people. He ordered his troops not burn the homes of civilians. But he did not stop his soldiers from destroying storehouses and other buildings.

After a 60-mile march to Bentonville, North Carolina, William met up with Johnston's troops. By this time, Johnston's army, like other Southern armies, was small and weakened from fighting. Still, Johnston fought fiercely. But William won the battle. He could not know that it would be his last battle of the Civil War.

Events were moving quickly. In Virginia, Grant won hard-fought battles, and General

Robert E. Lee finally surrendered his forces on April 9, 1865. Shortly after, William took the city of Raleigh, North Carolina, without a fight. On April 17, General Johnston asked to meet William. As the two commanders met, soldiers from each side rode out with white flags, a sign of peace. William and Johnston shook hands and began working on a document for Johnston's surrender and the end of the fighting. In the document, William agreed that the Union would not punish any Southerner who obeyed Union laws. He also agreed that the Union would allow Southern states to form local governments. These terms were beyond William's authority.

At the same time, William learned that President Lincoln had been shot and killed by a Southern sympathizer, John Wilkes Booth. Vice President Andrew Johnson was now president of the United States. When the new president and his secretary of war, Edwin Stanton, heard of William's terms, they were furious.

To his surprise, William was accused of betraying the Union. Stanton and President Johnson said he had acted selfishly. William responded by displaying his well-known temper to General Grant. According to Grant, William shouted and cursed all politicians. He explained that he had acted according to what he thought President Lincoln would have wanted. In the end, William had to offer harsher terms to General Johnston.

Despite his anger, William led his troops in a victory march in front of the White House on May 24. Riding a horse decorated with flowers, he passed before his family and his foster father, Thomas Ewing, who sat proudly in the audience. President Johnson did salute William as bands played and 75,000 spectators cheered. Less than a week later, William said good-bye to his men.

William ended the war as a major general, and twice Congress thanked him for his services. In the fall of 1865, William took command of army forces in the West. For the first time in many years, he lived with his family in St. Louis,

Missouri, in a house donated by citizens who were grateful for his Civil War service.

William's duties included protecting settlers who were rushing to take land in the Great Plains. His troops were also ordered to protect the men who were hurrying to build a railroad across the plains. But the Native Americans of the Great Plains were resisting the taking of their lands and the building of the railroad.

In late 1866, after Native Americans killed a group of soldiers, William wanted to attack. But President Johnson decided to try for peace, and he appointed William to a peace commission. Like so many Americans of the time, William did not believe that Indians belonged with white people. He thought they should give up their land to settlers. In a message to a group of chiefs, he wrote: "You must submit and do the best you can. If you continue fighting, you will all be killed."

In 1869, General Ulysses S. Grant was elected president. He immediately appointed William general of the U.S. army, and William moved

Crowds cheer as victorious Union troops march down Pennsylvania Avenue in Washington, D.C. William too was cheered and saluted by the president as he passed in review.

to Washington, D.C. As top commander of the army, William ordered his forces to protect settlers in the West at any cost.

Throughout the 1870s and 1880s, William gave many speeches and became a popular public speaker. He enjoyed attending operas, concerts,

Native Americans, like these pictured, fiercely resisted settlers on the Great Plains. As commander of the army in the West, William ordered Indians to submit or be destroyed.

and plays. He also wrote his memoirs, the story of his life and work. When it was published in 1885, the book became a bestseller. Everyone wanted to read about his battles and military strategies.

A very popular figure, William turned down several offers to run for president. One office he did gladly accept was president of the Society of the Army of Tennessee. He held that post from 1869 until the end of his life. He was also honored with degrees from the colleges of Dartmouth, Yale, and Princeton.

At the age of 64, William retired from the army and moved with his wife to New York City. A few months later, Ellen died from heart problems. Although William's grief was intense, he did keep up with his daily activities. But William was slowing down, and on February 14, 1891, he died.

William Tecumseh Sherman was remembered as a war hero and a brilliant general. He was mourned by thousands of people. At his military funeral, a trumpet played and soldiers from the Civil War fired three gun blasts in honor of his memory. William was buried in St. Louis next to his wife and his son Willie.

William's personality had a good side and a dark side. With his soldiers, he could show kindness and sensitivity, and he often chatted with them on long marches. But he also showed **prejudice**

William's last home was New York City, where he became a popular speaker and a best-selling writer. When he died in 1891, he was remembered as a war hero and brilliant general.

against African Americans and Native Americans. He did not feel they were equal to white people. He had refused to include free black soldiers in his army during the war until he was forced to, and he later ordered many attacks on Native Americans in the West. Although he is still criticized for his destruction in the South, his strategy helped the Union win and saved many Northern lives.

GLOSSARY

abolitionist–a person who wanted to do away with, or abolish, slavery

blockade–the closing of an area so that people and supplies cannot leave or enter

cadet–young man who enters a military academy to study

civilian–someone who does not serve in the military

Civil War–armed conflict between the North and the South in the United States from 1861–1865

compromise–an agreement in which both sides give up some of their wishes to settle an argument

Confederate States of America–those states that left the United States to form an independent nation

culture–the way of life of a group of people

demerit–mark against a person's record for poor behavior

entrenchment–a place surrounded by a trench for defense

forage–search for food

frontier–a place where settled land and wilderness meet

morale–a spirit, mood, or attitude

plantation–a large farm that usually raised one major crop, such as cotton

prejudice–an opinion formed about someone or a group without judging fairly

refugee–someone who flees an area for safety, especially in times of war

reinforcements–extra soldiers and supplies sent to battlefields

secede–to withdraw from a community or group in order to form a separate group

siege–the surrounding of a place by an army trying to capture it

skirmish–a small fight between groups

slavery–a system that takes away people's freedom and holds them against their will

strategy–plans and directions for military movements

truce–an agreement to stop fighting

Union–states that remained part of the United States during the Civil War

CHRONOLOGY

1820	Born Tecumseh Sherman on February 8 in Lancaster, Ohio.
1829	Father dies on June 24; moves into household of Thomas Ewing.
1830	Baptized by Ewings with first name William.
1836	Enters U.S. Military Academy at West Point in New York State.
1840	Graduates from West Point as second lieutenant; assigned to field service in Florida.
1846	Assigned to California at outbreak of the Mexican War.
1850	Marries Eleanor Boyle Ewing.
1853	Resigns military commission and works in California as a banker.
1857	Learns law and practices in Kansas.
1859	Appointed superintendent of Louisiana State Seminary of Learning and Military Academy.
1861	Rejoins the U.S. army with rank of colonel; Civil War begins.
1862	Distinguishes himself at Battle of Shiloh in Tennessee.
1863	Promoted to brigadier general; son Willie dies of fever.
1864	Marches to Atlanta, Georgia, and captures the city in September; Savannah, Georgia, falls to William's troops on December 21.

1865	Appointed to command U.S. armies in the West; becomes member of a peace commission to western Indians.
1869	Receives command of the entire U.S. army.
1884	Retires from the army.
1885	Publishes autobiography.
1891	Dies on February 14 in New York City.

CIVIL WAR TIME LINE

1860   Abraham Lincoln is elected president of the United States on November 6. During the next few months, Southern states begin to break away from the Union.

1861   On April 12, the Confederates attack Fort Sumter, South Carolina, and the Civil War begins. Union forces are defeated in Virginia at the First Battle of Bull Run (First Manassas) on July 21 and withdraw to Washington, D.C.

1862   Robert E. Lee is placed in command of the main Confederate army in Virginia in June. Lee defeats the Army of the Potomac at the Second Battle of Bull Run (Second Manassas) in Virginia on August 29–30. On September 17, Union general George B. McClellan turns back Lee's first invasion of the North at Antietam Creek near Sharpsburg, Maryland. It is the bloodiest day of the war.

1863   On January 1, President Lincoln issues the Emancipation Proclamation, freeing slaves in Southern states. Between May 1–6, Lee wins an important victory at Chancellorsville, but key Southern commander Thomas J. "Stonewall" Jackson dies from wounds. In June, Union forces hold the city of Vicksburg, Mississippi, under siege. The people of Vicksburg surrender on July 4. Lee's second invasion of the North during July 1–3 is decisively turned back at Gettysburg, Pennsylvania.

1864   General Grant is made supreme Union commander on March 9. Following a series of costly battles, on June 19 Grant successfully encircles Lee's troops in Petersburg, Virginia. A siege of the town lasts nearly a year. Union general William Sherman captures Atlanta on September 2 and begins the "March to the Sea," a campaign of destruction across Georgia and South Carolina. On November 8, Abraham Lincoln wins reelection as president.

1865   On April 2, Petersburg, Virginia, falls to the Union. Lee attempts to reach Confederate forces in North Carolina but is gradually surrounded by Union troops. Lee surrenders to Grant on April 9 at Appomattox, Virginia, ending the war. Abraham Lincoln is assassinated by John Wilkes Booth on April 14.

FURTHER READING

Clayton, Nancy, and Susan Spellman. *Civil War*. Los Angeles: Lowell House, 1999.

McAfee, Michael J. and John P. Langellier. *Billy Yank: The Uniform of the Union Army, 1861–1865*. Philadelphia: Chelsea House Publishers, 2000.

Sandler, Martin W., and James W. Billington. *Civil War: A Library of Congress Book*. New York: HarperCollins Publishers, 1996.

Savage, Douglas J. *The Soldier's Life in the Civil War*. Philadelphia: Chelsea House Publishers, 2000.

Whitelaw, Nancy. *William T. Sherman: Defender and Destroyer*. Greensboro, N.C.: Morgan Reynolds, 1996.

Free Library of Philadelphia website on the Civil War: http://www.historyplace.com/civilwar/index.html

INDEX

PICTURE CREDITS

ABOUT THE AUTHOR

HENNA R. REMSTEIN is a writer and communications professional in Philadelphia. Her last book for Chelsea House was a young adult biography of Barbara Walters.

Senior Consulting Editor **ARTHUR M. SCHLESINGER, JR.** is the leading American historian of our time. He won the Pulitzer Prize for his book *The Age of Jackson* (1945), and again for *A Thousand Days* (1965). This chronicle of the Kennedy Administration also won a National Book Award. He has written many other books, including a multi-volume series, *The Age of Roosevelt*. Professor Schlesinger is the Albert Schweitzer Professor of the Humanities at the City University of New York, and has been involved in several other Chelsea House projects, including the COLONIAL LEADERS series of biographies on the most prominent figures of early American history.

Remstein, Henna.

William Sherman.

DATE			